Character

Miriam: A grieving daughter in her mid-forties

Ste: Miriam's son in his early twenties

Amy: Daughter of Miriam in her mid twenties

SYNOPSIS:

Family dynamics are twisted and tested at a trying time for a grieving mother; Miriam who has just lost her father.

Miriam's son, Ste and daughter Amy each battle with their own form of grief, as they try to come together and stay strong, through a strange and trying time. Their Grandpa's past resurfaces in the form of an old welly that adds to the intrigue and mystery.

Scene 1

Living room with a small, out of place coffee table smack bang in the centre of the room. Ste is stood in front of it, concealing what is on the table. Amy and Miriam are sat down on a sofa. There are three condolence cards placed on the table, just behind the item that Ste is currently concealing.

Ste: (Holding out his hands, flabbergasted.) So this is it?

Amy: What did you expect?

Miriam: (Sombrely) I'm quite proud. This is how I remember him; slightly eccentric and unashamed of whom he was right until the end.

Ste: People who are stark raving bonkers usually are.

Miriam: I beg your pardon? Show some respect for your grandpa. He always used to stick up for you when you used to get picked on. Who was it who got your favourite football back off Jimmy Pickles on your seventh birthday?

Ste: Do I have to say thanks for that every year?

Amy: Ignore him; he was just banking on a monetary inheritance, so he could squander it all on Jim Beam in Liquid or that other overpriced club he patronizes.

Ste: (Moving away from the table; uncovering a mangy, caked in mud Wellington boot.) Seventy eight years on God's pleasant earth and, all you leave those who looked out for you for most of their lives is a scummy, grimy, slimy Wellington boot?

Amy: It's symbolic of how you treated him if you ask me.

Ste: I didn't ask you. You always butt in uninvited, trying to turn the attention on someone-else so we'll forget that you're as bad, probably even worse to be honest. I've had enough of you Sis', always putting people down.

(Ste goes over to the welly, picks it up and looks inside it. He then shakes it and puts it halfway on.)

Miriam: Stephen, what are you doing? Put it back, please?

Ste: Wait and see mum, I'm putting it to good use.

Amy: What are you going to do put it in your mouth?

Miriam: (Irritated.) Just give it a rest you two, will you? (Pause.) The welly was being put to good use where it was Stephen. It was helping me remember your grandpa!

Ste: Just look at it will you? All it's good for is flinging!

(Ste hops with the welly hanging off one of his feet, to the edge of the stage and flings the welly across the stage. It flies past Amy and Miriam who look shocked and a little frightened. Miriam gets up and collects the welly; dusts it off and puts it back on the table. Ste returns to stand by it, looking defiant.)

Amy: You're sick.

Ste: Oh come off it, Sis'. I was just paying my respects to grandpa in a practical way. We always had welly flinging contests. We were so good at one point; we were going to look to see if there was a grandpa and grandson category at the Highland fling?

Amy: (Angrily) I take it back what I said. You're not just sick, you're sick and twisted. You were being a disrespectful imbecile.

Miriam: Oh, Put a sock in it you two.

Ste: (Peering dismissively into the welly.) I don't think one's fit in there. The mud inside is that old it's set like concrete.

Miriam: Maybe to you it's just a manky old Welly. But, to me, it is much more and to your grandpa it obviously meant a great deal. It means that we obviously meant a great deal to him that he left it to us. So start appreciating what it really is, will you?

Ste: (Pointing demonstratively at the welly.) What else can it be? Look at it; I'm surprised his flat wasn't dawn raided by Environmental Health, years ago. The toxic fumes from it have destroyed more rain forests than acid rain.

Amy: Oh, here we go, those acting lessons mum paid for when you were twelve weren't wasted eh? Mr Drama King. Why don't you give us some of Hamlet's soliloquy whilst you're at it? You're mad enough to do it justice. (Pause)

(Ste climbs onto the table, picking up the welly, as he does so and knocking over one of the condolence cards. Miriam immediately gets up and puts the card back on the table, tuts and slaps Ste's leg, before sitting down looking indignant. Ste steadies himself, reaches out his hands as far as they will stretch and holds the welly out in-front of him, dramatically, as though it is a skull.)

Ste: (Feigning a Shakespearean tone and manner.) Alas, poor Albert, I knew him, Amy: a fellow of fine jest.

(Ste looks pleased with himself and climbs back down. Miriam looks shocked and Amy looks pitifully at Ste.)

Amy: That was pathetic and, your pitiful parody wasn't even from the soliloquy.

Ste: Who said it was meant to be?

Miriam: (With a hint of desperation in her voice.) Please show some respect Stephen, for grandpa's sake, if not, for mine?

Amy: You're wasting your breath mum. He's an inconsiderate little toad.

Ste: Think what you like, sis'. I was just making you focus on the welly, which is what grandpa obviously wanted! (Pause)

Amy: (Pointing to the Welly.) Anyway, I can see it and it's making me laugh.

Miriam: I hope it isn't, Amy?

Amy: I didn't mean it disrespectfully mum; I meant the state it's getting him into.

Ste: Listen to little Miss Hypocrite.

Amy: (Raising her voice, a little shocked.) Excuse me?

Miriam: Come on, both of you, please? We've just buried your grandpa. (Pause)

Ste: Amy?

Amy: What?

Ste; Come off it, you think I didn't see you?

Amy: See me what? Stop talking in riddles.

Miriam: Just have some respect both of you, for Pete's sake.

Amy: I thought his name was Albert?

Miriam: You know full well what I mean.

Ste: Stop changing the subject. I saw you, Amy, slyly slotting your luxury cruise brochures into the bin after the will reading. Shame on you!

(Miriam looks suspiciously at Amy then huffs in exasperation.)

Amy: You must be seeing things. Must be that fake Jim Beam you brought in the Roving Lamb, coming back to haunt you.

Miriam: Can we please just bury the squabbling? Remember what today's about!

Ste: Great turn of phrase, mum. I don't think I know what today is anymore?

Miriam: That's the problem with your generation, isn't it?

Ste: What is?

Miriam: (Raising her voice slightly.) The fact that if something isn't about you then you don't want to know.

Amy: Come on mum; we were just a bit shocked that's all. (Pointing to the Welly.) Admit it; you were surprised too, when you found out that this is all we have been left?

Ste: Where's the other one anyway?

Miriam: That was left to your uncle.

Ste: Was he as dismayed as we are?

Amy: Speak for yourself.

Ste: Quit it with the fake sincerity. You know I'm speaking for the both of us.

Miriam: (Smiling wryly.) A quite warming thought just occurred to me.

Amy: (Sincerely.) Go on, Mum.

Miriam: Maybe your grandpa did this to teach you two the true value of ...

Ste: (Interrupting.) The true value of what? That welly has no value.

Miriam: The true value of life, memories of everything, really!

Ste: Strange way of doing that isn't it? You'd have thought he'd want to look out for his family, wouldn't you?

Amy: (Puzzled) Are you sure that was everything we were left, mum?

Miriam: Yes, it is quite refreshing I think! Makes you focus on other things than squabbling over money like a pack of dirty hounds fighting over a bitch.

Ste: You should have pursued your poetry career mum.

Miriam: (Sternly.) Don't patronize me Stephen, it doesn't suit you.

Amy: Yeah, St-e-ph-en don't be patronizing.

Ste: Get stuffed, will you?

Amy: Have some respect, will you?

Ste: Yeah, like you did, not!

Miriam: Like neither of you have, really. (Pause. Sighs then looks pensively at the welly.) Do you not even have the slightest curiosity about where the welly has been? The places it has taken your grandpa to? (Pause)

Ste: No further than his backyard, the pub or the bookies is my bet.

Miriam: I think it's been further than that!

Amy: Where has it been, mum?

Miriam: (Exasperated.) Did you two not pay attention to those stories he told you about his trip the Amazon Rain Forest, to get a picture of a Macaw in its natural habitat for your gran? Four weeks it took him to get out there with Wilf Abbot. He was a real explorer your grandpa was! He always used to tell you two that story when you were younger.

Amy: Oh, I remember them now. I used to enjoy them.

Ste: Don't lie. You used to have to take four painkillers to get over the jaw ache you used to get from yawning.

Amy: Be careful St-e-ph-en.

Ste: Why should I? I'm sick of people telling me to be careful around you cos you're the sensitive one. You're as cold-hearted as the rest of us.

Amy: No I'm not.

Miriam: I'm getting weary of your bickering on today of all days.

Amy: I wasn't bickering mum. All I was saying was that he'd better be careful because I did care about grandpa and, I always listened to him. I remember and enjoyed all of his stories. (Pointing accusingly at Ste. Pause.) Unlike him, he used to slope off, pinch Grandpa's pellet gun and start hunting pigeons, whenever Grandpa started telling a story.

Ste: Come on then the stage is all yours…

Amy: I'd be glad to share one of his stories!

Miriam: Please do, that'd be nice of you, Amy.

(Amy stands up looking proudly at the welly and clears her throat dramatically.)

Amy: My favourite one; is when grandpa and Wilf Abbott went to Mexico in order to collect some Agave plants to make their own Tequila. A scorpion crawled inside grandpa's wellies, but because the wellies were two sizes too big for him. There was enough room for Grandpa to wrestle it with his toe and, after a long struggle he managed to crush it. (Pause; smiling) You wouldn't even see Bear Grylls doing that, would you? (Sitting back down.)

Ste: That's a lame story; you haven't even tried with that one. If you're going to make something up; at least make something up that's half believable.

Miriam: It is true, I heard him tell her, I don't know where you had gone?

Ste: It's probably true that he told her the story, but you know as well as I do that the nearest he got to Mexico was when he accidentally sat on a cactus at the garden centre, a few years back!

Amy: Did we ever find out who put that cactus on the chair? I think I have an idea!

Ste: He put it there himself, when he took it off the table to put his wellies there!

Miriam: I remember that. Five hours we were waiting in A & E. He was so patient!

Ste: He just complained all the time, remember? (Pause) He even complained about the food. I mean, I know that's usually acceptable with hospital food, but not when you pinch a pregnant lady's lasagne, surely?

Miriam: As he explained to you at the time; he thought she'd left it.

Amy: Anyway, how do you know much about that trip to the hospital? You went down the pub and only came back when it was time to go, remember?

Ste: Only after an hour or so. Anyway, you came with me, remember?

Miriam: The both of you stayed away for as long as you could!

Amy: I only went to keep an eye on Stephen!

Miriam: It doesn't matter now; I am not dwelling on things like that today. I want to remember the good things!

Amy: You're right, mum. It doesn't matter, he'll never change anyway.

Ste: Some of us don't need to, ta very much!

Miriam: (Pause.) That's what makes me so proud of your grandpa.

Amy: What's does, mum?

Miriam: The fact that he didn't change and remained true to who he was, right until the end! (Pause.)

Ste: That's what I meant to ask!

Miriam: What's that?

Amy: Can I go The Roving Lamb now? Is all that he usually asks.

Ste: Cheers for that, Amy. Cynicism's a disease, you know?

Amy: Well, you should know.

Ste: Where is Wilf Abbott? That's what I meant to ask before I was rudely interrupted! Could he not make it today?

Miriam: I don't know. We tried phoning him in Thurso and sent him two letters, but we didn't get a reply. He has sent a condolence card (pointing to one of the cards on the table). I'll send him a letter thanking him for that and tell him that he is always welcome to come and visit us. It's really good that he's been in touch and that he's thinking of grandpa.

Ste: They hardly spoke to each other in the last twenty or so years, he used to snap at me and change the subject, whenever I mentioned Wilf's name!

Miriam: Oh, stop stirring, Stephen. They were still friends, distance just got in the way. They have been friends for fifty years or more!

Ste: Not friendly enough for Wilf to come to his funeral, though?

Miriam: He is probably off exploring.

Amy: That's the best way to remember grandpa, I think. (Pause)

Exploring intrepidly with Wilf. It perks me up, remembering him that way.

Ste: Creep.

Amy: Think what you like, Ste.

Ste: Anyway, Mum. You told me and grandpa often told me that he had arthritis in his early thirties. He's used it as an excuse not to do any chores ever since.

Amy: Cynicism's a disease, you know, Ste?

Ste: Just stating the facts!

Miriam: Grandpa and Wilf weren't as close later on in their lives, people drift apart, but they were still friends. (Pause.)

Ste: Anyway, I was just gonna ask: how did grandpa do all this exploring when he always complained of his arthritis?

Miriam: He never let it stop him living his life.

Amy: No he didn't, you would, Ste. You'd be claiming more benefits than Wauneta Slob, if you had something like that and, your new address would be The Roving Lamb.

Ste: I really don't know where I'd be in life without your support, Amy? (Pause.)

(Ste marches up and down, looks thoughtful for a moment and then wanders over to the table. He starts looking at the condolence cards, whilst Amy and Miriam continue talking.)

Miriam: (Pause.) You can be cruel to him, sometimes. Your Grandpa always used to notice you two niggling at each other.

Amy: I do try mum, but he's impossible sometimes. I just don't like him criticising me and grandpa, all the time.

Miriam: He hasn't been it's been a difficult day for us all. Don't you think?

Amy: I suppose, he's always like this though.

Miriam: You're both as bad as each other, sometimes.

Ste: (Engrossed in reading the condolence card that he's still holding; he speaks without lifting his head up.) I'm still here you know? (Pause) I can hear every stinging word you say about me. I haven't crawled into my grave as well, even though you probably wish I had?

Amy: Oh go back to your comics.

(Ste ignores her, focusing on reading the card in front of him. He then puts it down and picks up another of the condolence cards; concentrating obliviously on reading it.)

Miriam: Amy?

Amy: What, mum?

Miriam: You do need to give your brother a break. He's reading the condolence cards.

Amy: He's probably checking to see if anyone has put any money in any of them?

Miriam: That was uncalled for.

Amy: Sorry, it's been an emotional day. Were there only three cards?

Miriam: Yes, your grandpa kept himself to himself over the last few years. (Pause) And, you know what the post is like; we'll probably get another half a dozen tomorrow!

Amy: Yeah, you're probably right. He was very popular with the dominoes team!

Miriam: He was a dab hand with the dominoes. I used to love watching him playing dominoes; he always looked so focused, yet contented.

Amy: I'm really glad that Wilf was able to send a card, anyway, even if he couldn't make it today.

Miriam: Me too, hopefully we'll hear from him soon.

Amy: We'll probably get a postcard from him from Madagascar next week!

Ste: (Gasping, then raising his voice in shock!) Holy mackerel!

Amy: Oh, Mr Drama King's back again!

Ste: Have you read this card from Wilf yet?

(Ste shakes the card nervously, appearing a little flustered.)

Miriam: No, I haven't had a moment to myself yet, it only came this morning. (Pause, looking worried.)

Ste: I really think you need to read it, both of you.

Miriam: Why? What does it say, Stephen?

Ste: Brace yourselves. I'll read it out:

"Dear Albert, I sincerely hope that whoever reads these next few words of mine?

Appreciates the irony that these words mean that I have communicated to you more in death than I have in the last 20 years! Maybe, I was a little too harsh on you, but what you did hurt me. I learnt early on in our friendship to tolerate you hiding dominoes whenever we played.

However, I could not see it in my heart to forgive you for the sly act of stealing my wellies in Scarborough, all those years ago, whilst Mable and I were skinny dipping. Had you just told me that you wanted them (though, I could not think why you would you want them given that my athlete's foot was at its worst?) we could have come to some arrangement.

There have been times over the years. Whereby, I wanted to make contact with you, I always felt that it was you who had to make the first attempt to patch things up. I also knew that your stubbornness would prevent you from doing this. I've appreciated your stubbornness over the years. None more so than your refusal to vacate the cinema when we were asked to leave, we'd never have seen the end of 'Gone with the Wind'!

In learning of your passing, I now realise that friendship is important than material things. I sincerely hope that those close to you draw comfort from the following statement:

I now forgive you Albert Flintlock!

Rest in peace.

Your friend,

Wilf"

The end

HOBBY
HORSE

Characters:

Stu: A Wigan Athletic fan and civil servant

Kerry: Member of The Verve tribute band, in her late twenties

Martin: Junior Rugby League Coach in his late 20s/ early 30s

Tina: Athlete, student and member of Bitter Sweet

Katy: Member of bar staff from London

Joe: An intrepid local journalist

Chris: Unemployed and down-to--earth.

Latics Fan1: Enthusiastic for his team and Over 30 years old

Latics fan2: Any age

Tacky Olympic Bracelet Pedlar: Female; over 40 years old and of a world-weary disposition

SYNOPSIS:

The action takes place in the run up to the London 2012 Olympics in the town of Wigan, north west England.

The colourful residents ponder, for different reasons, what the forthcoming Olympics means to and for them? Pre-existing rivalries and jealousy starts to bubble to the surface, as they do so.

ALL CHANGE

Characters:

Faye: **A tightly wound ticket seller in her 30s**

Lucy: **An ambitious, curious bank manager in her late twenties**

SYNOPSIS:

Lucy has tirelessly climbed up the banking ladder relying on punctuality, ambition and innovation. These three qualities have never let her down. Add to this a chameleon-like ability to adapt to change and she is seemingly unflappable.

One idle Tuesday morning, everything Lucy values seems to be conspiring against her! The human aspect of this conspiracy, confronts her in the form of Faye. Faye's job has been the ultimate in tedium and routine. Suddenly, her job is changing; for the better, in her mind and, she now has something to believe in, with unrelenting conviction.

OCCUPA-
TIONAL
HAZARD

Characters:

Pete: A Marketing Team Leader In His Early Twenties.

Boomerang: In His Mid-Twenties.

SYNOPSIS:

A play set outside a popular pub; The Frying Frisbee. Two strangers are literally flung together and an unlikely alliance begins to develop.

Troubles are laid out and analysed and each character begins to see things from the other's perspective. Illuminating the point that the pub setting (or outside of it, in this case!) is often the place whereby personal barriers are broken down and the stiff upper lip stance is buried for an evening.

Pete is sat with his head in his hands outside a pub called The Flying Frisbee. He pauses, looks up to the sky in desperation, whilst the chorus to the Beck song, 'Loser' can be heard from inside the pub. He shrugs dismissively and places his head back in his hands. He is then disturbed by a crashing sound, as Boomer falls spectacularly through the doors. He lands right at Pete's feet. Before bouncing back upright, posturing and gesturing, making his first comments to the door that he has just been flung through.

Boomerang: (Animated.) All right, all right no need for the rough stuff, Max. I was going quietly. Get back to Phoenix Nights, you idiot.

Pete: If that's quietly? Then I wouldn't wanna hear you making a fuss.

Boomerang: Oh, you're still here are you? I thought you'd be off licking your wounds?

Pete: Not my style.

Boomerang: (Sitting down next to Pete) It should be. Given what you said to that bouncer on your way out and, what you said to that meat-head; your girlfriend?

Pete: Yeah, she was my girlfriend.

Boomerang: Thought so, then what you said that meat-head your girlfriend was flirting provocatively with. You had some balls to say what you did, mate.

Pete: I reckon I was quite lenient in the circumstances.

Boomerang: Well, excuse me Judge Rinder.

Pete: Uh?

Boomerang: The presiding judge in the O.J. Simpson trial.

Pete: Right.

Boomerang: I ain't wasting time explaining me puns on a Saturday night.

Pete: You mean there's gonna be more?

Boomerang: You never know your luck. It is lottery night.

Pete: That's very astute of you, pointing that out.

Boomerang: You should thank your lucky stars that your bonus balls are still intact.

Pete: I'll remember that.

Boomerang: Anyway.

Pete: Anyway, what?

Boomerang: I was just saying, before I got distracted by my own wit.

Pete: (Sighing) Go on, tell me. I know you're dying to.

Boomerang: About the circumstances.

Pete: What about them?

Boomerang: Do you think those guys give a damn about the circumstances?

Pete: I do. And, I don't give a rat's ass what they think.

Boomerang: You made that clear on your way out too, mate.

(Pete stands up looking agitated, determined and angry.)

Pete: You know what?

Boomerang: What mate?

Pete: I'm gonna make it even clearer now, cos I'm going back in.

Boomerang: (Putting his palm on Pete's chest) Wait mate, don't be hasty.

(Pete pushes Boomerang's hand away and rushes back through the door into the pub. Almost straight away he flies out of the door again, with more force than Boomerang did. Also, he lands further away than him too. Boomerang picks Pete up, dusts him off and sits him back down.)

Pete: Go on, say it: I told you so.

Boomerang: There's no point mate, I'm not one for saying things I don't need to.

Pete: Good.

Boomerang: As long as you're OK?

Pete: I am, Ta.

Boomerang: Anyway, I was saying that I thought you made yourself clear the first time. Especially as two meat-heads were choking you like a chicken and dragging you towards the door.

Pete: Like a sack of unwanted spuds?

Boomerang: Manure.

Pete: Eh?

Boomerang: Like a sack of manure, I was gonna say. Or a word to that effect!

Pete: Either way.

Boomerang: Yeah, both work. (Pause)

Pete: Were they still at it, flirting when you left?

Boomerang: I dunno mate, it was crowded and I wasn't exactly paying attention.

Pete: Yeah; full of pricks.

Boomerang: Now, now.

Pete: What?

Boomerang: No need to hate the world, mate. You don't know half of the people in there, I bet?

Pete: I don't know you?

Boomerang: Oh yeah, how remiss of me. I'm Boomerang. (He shakes Pete's hand)

Pete: Boomerang?

Boomerang: I guess that's one of the reasons why I kept that nickname; Every time I tell it to someone, it comes back at me.

Pete: That right?

Boomerang: But don't worry, you can just call me Boomer if you like?

Pete: No, it's OK, I think I can manage the whole three syllables. Thanks anyway though, Boomerang.

Boomerang: Not a problem. And you're?

Pete: Peed off. That's what I am. (Pause) Pete's the name though.

Boomerang: Peed off Pete, eh?

Pete: For now.

Boomerang: I'm sure you'll bounce back.

Pete: You bet I will.

Boomerang: It doesn't help to stay angry mate. I've learnt that if nothing else over the years.

Pete: I won't, don't worry about that, Boomer.

Boomerang: (Smiling wryly) Why don't you head home mate? You'll catch the end of Match of the Day, if you hurry. I'll walk some of the way with you, if you like? I'm gonna go to The Crown or The White Lion or Margot's. Not decided yet, so I can walk whichever way you like. I'm like that me, salt of the earth.

Pete: I'm good for a bit, thanks anyway though.

Boomerang: Your funeral, I guess.

Pete: One man's funeral is another man's party.

Boomerang: Good philosophy. I've gotta say you seem very lucid, seeing as you seemed to be knocking 'em back like Amy Winehouse at a Brits after show party, in there.

Pete: I'll take that as a compliment, eh?

Boomerang: (He reaches into the inside pocket of his jacket and pulls out a bottle of beer. He undoes the lid with a key and hands it to Pete.) Here, take this as a compliment, I don't share my precious nectar with just anyone. The party doesn't have to stop when you're with Boomer.

Pete: Cheers. (He raises the bottle in acknowledgment of Boomerang and takes a large sip.)

Boomerang: Your welcome.

Pete: How in the name of Charlotte Church did you manage to get this out? They wouldn't even let me bring a bottle of water out with me. (Pause) Why did you get thrown out?

Boomerang: You saw the queues in there at the bar, didn't you?

Pete: I did.

Boomerang: Well I thought, if it's good enough for ASDA, it's good enough for here. So I went round and started serving myself.

Pete: Serving or helping yourself?

Boomerang: A little from column A, a little from column B.

Pete: (Smiling) Nice style, I like it.

Boomerang: They didn't notice until I went for a pint. Like most petty criminals; I got greedy that's how I got caught, you know the rest of the story.

Pete: Greed is the downfall of many a man, if you ask me?

Boomerang: Greed and envy is a lethal cocktail too mate.

Pete: What are you implying?

Boomerang: Nothing, mate.

Pete: My story's about honour and pride.

Boomerang: Honour and pride can lead you into no end of bother. Just ask Napoleon.

Pete: I will do, was he in there tonight?

Boomerang: He might've been, it's a busy pub.

Pete: Can I ask you a question, Boomerang?

Boomerang: Of course you can, mate. I'm an open book.

Pete: You're not in marketing by any chance, are you?

Boomerang: Not a chance mate. Is that what you do?

Pete: Yeah, why; what's wrong with that?

Boomerang: Not a bean, mate. It's just that I ain't suitable to join the Dolly Parton crew, I'm afraid. I'm just not cut out for it.

Pete: Eh?

Boomerang: Workin' nine till five. It's just not for me. It suits some people.

Pete: Like me, you mean?

Boomerang: Like most people really.

Pete: Yeah.

Boomerang: I mean, you seem to have it sussed.

Pete: Do I?

Boomerang: Yeah, you soak up the pressure in the week. Then you come to places like The Flying Frisbee and then let off steam at the weekend. Maybe even the odd night in the week too, on a special occasion?

Pete: Do you think it's that simple?

Boomerang: I'm not saying it's simple, mate. Just that I'm not one of those people who can bottle all the pressure up and then let off steam later. I wish I could, I'd be heading up a Microsoft Office somewhere in the States if I could. Wouldn't I? (Smiling then taking a large sip of beer.)

Pete: You do make it sound so simple, though. Have you ever tried it?

Boomerang: Not for a long time.

Pete: Why not for a long time?

Boomerang: Like I said because I'm not suited to it.

Pete: You don't have to be suited to it, do you? But it makes sense to do it.

Boomerang: To you, maybe it does.

Pete: Why doesn't it make sense to you, Boomerang?

Boomerang: To be honest, I just don't think I have the same needs as you, that's all.

Pete: What needs would they be, exactly?

Boomerang: The need to be wanted.

Pete: Wanted by who? There are no posters on trees, lampposts and bus stops with my picture on them, if that's what you mean?

Boomerang: I think you know that it wasn't mate. Although there might be after tonight?

Pete: (Pause, he looks thoughtful and then enlightened) I've got it!

Boomerang: Got what? Is it contagious, mate?

Pete: The reason why you're mysterious and try to deflect all the focus onto me. It took me a while, but you can understand that I've been a bit distracted with my thoughts, can't you?

Boomerang: I don't know what you're on about mate?

Pete: Don't you, Boomer?

Boomerang: I'm afraid I don't.

Pete: You applied for a job in marketing or some high flying equivalent and you didn't get it. Now you spend your time trying to bring the rest of us down to your level.

Boomerang: (Laughs feigning hysterics) That's what I like about you rat race entrants; you think that everyone who's not like you has tried to be like you and failed.

Pete: (Perturbed) I'm not wrong in your case though, am I, Boomerang?

Boomerang: It all depends on interpretation, doesn't it?

Pete: Does it? (Pause)

Boomerang: You're right.

Pete: I knew I was!

Boomerang: About one thing!

    Pete: Eh?

Boomerang: I did have a nine til' five job, just like you mate!

    Pete: Oh Yeah?

Boomerang: Yeah and, I was good at it and all, too good!

    Pete: I don't understand you, Boomerang. How can you be too good at a job? You'd be running the place if you were.

Boomerang: Aaahh, the naivety of a University education and a graduate job.

    Pete: I'm not naive.

Boomerang: Let me clear it up for you?

    Pete: By all means, Boomer.

Boomerang: Pretty much straight after I finished school in order to help my agoraphobic mum after my dad had left us, I went straight into work. I was counting ready meals in a warehouse on ten hour shifts.

    Pete: Hotpots?

Boomerang: You what?

    Pete: Was it hotpots that you were counting?   **Boomerang:**   Hotpots were involved, but I think I counted more shepherd's pies to be honest with you.

    Pete: Yeah? I prefer Hotpots myself. My Nan used to make the best Hotpot ever.

Boomerang: Well, it wouldn't take much to beat the hotpots I counted anyway, mate.

    Pete: A good hotpot is always homemade, if you ask me?

Boomerang: Anyway, it wasn't about that. I only counted them at first. I didn't test them, mate.

    Pete: Oh right, carry on then.

Boomerang: Anyway, my point is. I was the best in the warehouse at counting ready meals. I was quick, punctual and well mannered. All the skills necessary for the job!

Pete: It certainly sounds like a great job, how do I apply?

Boomerang: I don't know. I'm not working there anymore.

Pete: Oh right.

Boomerang: Anyway, to cut a long story short....

Pete: Please do mate.

Boomerang: (Oblivious to Pete's last remark) I was promoted to recording and analysing the results of the counting. Then, after only a few months I was made a shift leader, looking after people who did the job I started off doing.

Pete: Don't tell me you own the factory now?

Boomerang: Not quite mate. Two weeks later I had to find out why two boxes of ready meals per shift were going missing.

Pete: I bet it was the hotpots that were going missing and not the shepherd's pies?

Boomerang: I can't remember. That's not important anyway, mate.

Pete: Fair enough Boomer, anyway, you can't be seen to uphold pilfering, someone with your moral fibre.

Boomerang: I'd listen to this last bit mate.

Pete: I'm all ears.

Boomerang: I found out who it was and dismissed them straight away. Or summarily is the legal term they use isn't it?

Pete: I think you're right, it is, Boomer.

Boomerang: Only a few weeks later I found out that the guy's wife had Leukaemia and he was looking after her, working 5 twelve hour shifts and looking after five young children.

Pete: You weren't to know that.

Boomerang: I would if I'd have asked him? Or if I'd have taken time to get to know the circumstances.

Pete: What happened to him?

Boomerang: Last thing I heard, he was refused benefits because he was sacked from his previous job and got behind with the rent. He got evicted from his house, with his family. Try as I did, I couldn't find out what happened to him, after that? (Pause. Boomer looks melancholic and reflective.) Do you ever think about the impact of the decisions you make at work? How they can affect other people's lives?

Pete: I can't really say that I have mate. So, I take it you don't work there anymore?

Boomerang: You take it right, mate.

Pete: What exactly is it that you do for a living now, then?

(Boomerang gets up trying to listen to what is going on inside the pub. He holds out his hand indicating for Pete to stop talking.)

Boomerang: Hold on a minute mate, this is my tune.

Pete: What is it? I can't hear it properly.   (He cocks his ear towards the pub so that he can hear the music.)

(Boomerang starts dancing like Bez from the Happy Mondays. Shaking his air maracas and singing some of the words to 'Step On', by the Happy Mondays.)

Boomerang: (Singing enthusiastically and a little out of key.) "He's gonna step on you again, he's gonna step on you. He's gonna step on you again, he's gonna step on you. You're twistin' my melon man, you know you talk so hip man. You're twistin' my melon man."

(He sits back down, putting his arm around Pete and rubbing his shoulder, briefly.)

Pete: That was great, Boomer. But ...

Boomerang: But, what?

Pete: It was The Stone Roses they were playing; 'Made Of Stone'.

Boomerang: Are you sure?

Pete: Sure I'm sure. It's the song that was playing at the work's Christmas party when I chatted up Kirsty for the first time. A fat lot of good it did me in the end, eh?

Boomerang: (Shaking his head in disbelief.) I could have sworn I was listening to the Happy Mondays then.

Pete: Sorry to disappoint you.

Boomerang: I'm always doing that. Once I get a song in my head, I can hear it no matter what else playing. It used to get quite embarrassing at family parties when they'd be playing Elvis and I'd be singing and dancing along to The Who. (Pause) Kirsty, is that the girl in there?

Pete: Yeah.

Boomerang: Aaaahh, so you two work together?

Pete: We do, unfortunately.

Boomerang: What is it that you market, exactly?

Pete: Music! Any band that's worth their salt, we promote. That's the motto at Jive PR anyway.

Boomerang: Sounds fun that mate.

Pete: Yeah, so does skiing.

Boomerang: You what?

Pete: Skiing sounds fun, but it's dangerous.

Boomerang: Are you saying you're job's dangerous, mate?

Pete: You wouldn't understand, Boomer.

Boomerang: Oh no, m8, I have full sympathy for you. I fully understand.

Pete: You do?

Boomerang: Yeah, paper cuts can be nasty, especially if you get them in the wrong places. (Pause) Sheesh, I can just imagine Chilean miner's saying to themselves "God, that Pete has a tough job at Jive PR."

Pete: Don't knock someone's job until you've done it yourself, Boomer.

Boomerang: So, you and Kirsty met over a Funeral for a Friend poster, eh?

Pete: (Smiling) Yeah, something like that. Nearly a year ago, now.

Boomerang: It's gonna be an occupational hazard bumping into her at work on Monday, ain't it mate?

Pete: Yeah, I suppose it will. We work in different parts of the office now, mind. I don't need to have much to do with her, so it won't be too bad. I certainly won't go looking for her.

Boomerang: I know all about them.

Pete: What? Ex-girlfriends?

Boomerang: No, occupational hazards.

Pete: Oh yeah?

Boomerang: But I won't bore you with my piffling troubles.

Pete: Are you suggesting that I've been boring you?

Boomerang: Not all mate. Why are you being so defensive? Are you trying to get a job at the back for United?

Pete: (Smiling and shaking his head) You did warn me that there'd be more lame puns. Didn't you?

Boomerang: There's nothing lame about my humour. The other kids used to give me their lunch money just for telling them jokes.

Pete: That's not really true, is it Boomer?

Boomerang: Well, I used to get their lunch money, anyway.

Pete: I bet you did.

Boomerang: (Pause) What's your plan?

Pete: What do you mean, plan?

Boomerang: What are you going to do now? You can't just stay here waiting for another confrontation, like a guest on The Jeremy Kyle show. Can you?

Pete: Sounds like a good plan to me.

Boomerang: It's not a plan, it's kamikaze mission. You tried a kamikaze mission earlier on, remember?

Pete: Oh yeah, don't remind. Oh you just did!

Boomerang: Revenge is a dish best served cold and you're steamin' right now.

Pete: It's just wrong what happened to me. Don't you think?

Boomerang: It's more wrong if you let it niggle at you like a maggot at a pound of rotting flesh. (Pause; Pete looks pensive.) Have you heard of Natural Justice?

Pete: No, what sort of music do they play?

Boomerang: Eh? No it's an erm. What do ya call it? A concept.

Pete: No I know, Boomer. I'm just showing what it's like to be on the receiving end of a lame pun.

Boomerang: You're right there. That was lame.

Pete: I thought it was quite good.

Boomerang: I think it's good you're showing signs that you're ready to move on.

Pete: On where?

Boomerang: To The Red Lion.

Pete: I suppose you're right, no use hanging around here.

Boomerang: No suppose about it; you know it makes sense.

Pete: Why?

Boomerang: Cos I'm gonna buy you a drink that's why.

Pete: My luck's changing already.

Boomerang: More than you know, mate.

Pete: You're talking in riddles again, Boomer.

Boomerang: (He gets up confidently) I've gotta admit mate, I did only tell you a half-truth when I said that I would buy you a drink.

Pete: You're not welching out on a round before we've even got to the pub are you?

Boomerang: Would I do something like that?

Pete: I'm not entirely sure, you're a bit of a mystery Boomer.

Boomerang: It's good to have mystery, sometimes.

Pete: Yeah, I suppose that's why Sherlock Holmes is so popular?

Boomerang: You're probably right, mate. Anyway, Like I said, I'm not going to you a drink, but....

Pete: But, what? (Pause)

Boomerang: Well, the person actually paying for your drink is the guy who kindly escorted you and then me to the door and through it, earlier on. (He smiles shiftily and produces a wallet, shaking it confidently.)

Pete: You stole that bouncer's wallet? Is that why you're touring the pubs? You're hard-core you are, Boomer.

Boomerang: Not really, you do what you have to too survive. Besides I've a soft side to me.

Pete: Oh yeah?

Boomerang: Yeah.

(Boomerang smiles and reaches into his jacket again, pulling out another wallet. Pete looks a bit bemused, as though he recognizes it. He flings the 2nd wallet down to Pete, who catches it.)

Boomerang: Here you go. You can have yours back. You're alright you are, Pete.

(Boomerang strolls confidently off the stage. Pete smiles, shakes his head and then gets up and follows him.)

The end

ABOUT THE AUTHOR

David Adair

A writing enthusiast who has written plays and articles aplenty.

The highlight regarding playwriting came in 2012; writing and co-producing a play entitled 'Hobby Horse.' This play centred around people from Wigan and their reaction to the 2012 London Olympics.

David has 20+ years experience writing freelance articles for a range of social news websites including www.blastingnews.com.

A lover of wildlife and a desire to inform and educate has been the motivation for writing this story.

Printed in Great Britain
by Amazon

67211531R00031